For my sister Karen and her wonderful ears x – CP

Published in the UK by Scholastic, 2024
1 London Bridge, London, SE1 9BG
Scholastic Ireland, 89E Lagan Road, Dublin Industrial Estate,
Glasnevin, Dublin, D11 HP5F



HB ISBN 978 0702 32371 3
PB ISBN 978 0702 33006 3

A CIP catalogue record for this book is available from the British Library.



Printed in China
Paper made from wood grown in sustainable forests and other controlled sources

1 3 5 7 9 10 8 6 4 2



www.scholastic.co.uk

# The Little Worried Caterpillar

Christine Pym

SCHOLASTIC

Deep down in the plants, at the first light of day,
Little Green sprang awake and got ready to play.

She searched for her friends through the low leafy ground,
but her caterpillar chums were nowhere to be found.

“Up here, Little Green,” came a faraway cry.
There were her friends, soaring up in the sky!

No longer caterpillars
crawling on leaves.
They were butterflies now,
flying high on the breeze.

"We have changed!" they all cheered.
"You'll be next, there's no doubt!"

Little Green gulped as fear started to sprout.

The worry set in, like a small, shooting seed.
And started to spread like a wild growing weed.

Green's friends were so pleased
with the wings they had grown.
But Green loved who she was
and she feared the unknown.

She liked her short legs and her zingy green skin.
Green worried, with wings, she'd feel different within.

So she asked the Big Greens,
as they munched a lush meal,
"I'm worried," she said.
"How does change make you feel?"

"Worried?
Don't be silly!"

"To change
is exciting!"

"We're born to transform
and the skies are inviting!"

Green knew that was true but she worried some more.
She wandered away feeling worse than before.

"You're worried?" buzzed Bee,
"oh, I know just the cure!

The smell of this rose,
it will help you for sure!"

So Little Green sniffed
and her eyes opened wide . . .

"It's working!" she gasped
as the scent whirled inside.

But then her eyes watered,
she braced with a squeeze . . .

. . . and out came a startling, trumpet-like sneeze!

Then the worry came back, just as big and as strong.
Little Green murmured, "There's still something wrong!"

"You're worried?" said Shrew as he nibbled a treat.
"Just bite on this berry and life will be sweet!"

So Little Green did.

With a burst of belief
she ate ALL the berries . . .

. . . but found no relief.

"It's hopeless," thought Green as she took one last lick,
"I still feel so worried . . . and now I feel sick!"

Little Green had no clue
for what else she could try.

She felt lost and alone
so she started to cry.

She curled into a ball and shut her eyes tight.

When a kind voice behind her said . . .

"Are you all right?"

Green's little lip quivered, she shook, all upset,
"I'm so scared and so worried!" she said, in a fret.

"You're worried?" said Rabbit. "Please share all your fears.
I'll listen," she said, "with my two pointy ears."

So Little Green spoke
and with every word,
Rabbit, very quietly,
listened and **heard**.

"It's scary," Green sighed,
"I have not changed before!
I'm worried I won't feel
like **me** any more."

"Yes, I understand," Rabbit said. "Sure enough,
to leave what we know can feel tricky and tough!"

"Though change is a thing that we all must go through.
Just know this," Rabbit said, "you will always be you!"

All of a sudden, Green relaxed, she felt good.
Her worries were out and a friend understood.

Green thanked her new friend,
with a fluttery heart,

"I'm ready," she said,
"for my journey to start."

Green found a good spot, in the leaves thick and deep,
and made preparations for her magical sleep.
She created a beautiful soft, silky spin,
and when she was done, she lay happy within.

Safely tucked up inside, all was calm, all was right.
And when Green emerged she felt . . .

…floaty
and
light!

And from that day on, bright, bold Butterfly Green,
helped all with a worry to be heard and feel **seen**.